Not Your Princess

By Jessica Mitzel

Dedication

To all survivors.

Prologue

I am not your princess.

I am not your anything.

Not anymore.

I used to be a lot of things to you;

    your friend's daughter,

    your toy,

    your secret.

Hopefully now I am only a regret.

I suppose I should go back, start at the beginning. Problem is, I don't really know what should be considered the start of it all. Uncertainty, story of my life, at least one story. The real one is much more serious.

Chapter 1

I was a girl pretending to be a princess.

I was born in February, a winter baby, born to snow, ice, and more snow. Luckily I was blessed a warm family to keep the chills at bay. My parents had hoped and prayed for a baby girl, and as I've been told, "God answered our prayers, and gave us the perfect daughter." So let me fill you in on a few things:

1. I am not religious. Religion plays a big part in this story.

2. I am far from perfect. Trust me on this one.

My loving family, however well intentioned, had bigger priorities. My father worked a lot. My mother went back to college, taking night classes when I was young. My older brothers wanted nothing to do with an annoying younger sister. I lived in a town of only 100 people, and there was no one my age. Very often, I was left to entertain myself. I created magical fantasies, made up stories of faraway lands to fill the voids I had building inside me. Little did I know then that these voids would only continue to grow.

I was lonely, desperate for a friend to confide in, someone to love. This longing paired with my naivety made me an easy target, the perfect prey.

He was always in my life. Since I was born he was there, just like my family. With my father so distant, that man became a surrogate, filling the vacant position in my life referred to as "dad". He was everyone's friend. He brought children presents and remembered anniversaries. He was religious, and above all else, trusted.

He began what I would later learn is called grooming. At the time though, it just seemed like someone cared. He brought me presents and candy on a weekly basis. Licorice was my favorite. Now it makes me gag. He gave me so many hugs. Presents were abundant. Dresses, necklaces, butterfly hair clips. Later he would give me a flute. All just different ways to make me feel special. He would talk to me after church for over an hour every week, and let me help him clean up after mass. For the first time in my life I felt like a priority. I wasn't just the afterthought anymore. Not to him. I was loved. That was all it took to capture my heart. Little did I know then that his love would come at a price.

Chapter 2

I was a little girl in big bird pajamas.

It started as young as I can remember, and for a while it was innocent enough, as I'm sure most abuse is. An "accidental" touch in a bad spot. Tickling that got a little too close to "no no areas". Little things that made me uncomfortable. But obviously they must have been accidents, so I said nothing. I guess he was testing me, to see how far he could go. I was so afraid of losing him that I let him go as far as he wanted. He started slipping his hands under my clothes, and me, younger than 5, didn't know I could do anything to make it stop. So it continued.

I thought the things we did were normal. I thought that everyone had someone that did those things to them. He told me I was special, called me his princess. He made me believe that he really cared for me. Call it childhood naivety or call it stupidity, but I honestly believed he loved me. When I was six he promised to marry me. I held onto that promise much longer than I should have. Those four words echoed in my head and grabbed tight to my heart, spinning a web of lies that I got all tangled up in. Those four words would be my undoing every time I spoke with someone about my abuse. It took me years to even call it abuse. For the longest time it was just the way life was. Nothing more, nothing less.

I hated what he did to me. I hated the pain, the way he made me feel. I hated the secrets he threatened me to keep. But at the same time, I reveled in it. I loved the attention. I would happily put up with the sex in exchange for the undivided attention. In exchange for what I thought was love.

You close the door behind you and lean up against it, crossing your arms across your chest. You stand that way for a while, just observing. I can hear the adults playing cards downstairs, and momentarily I wonder why you aren't with them. But then the thought is gone. I ignore you, continuing to play with my dolls. Eventually you speak, asking for permission to play with me. I get so excited, running over, grabbing your arm, and dragging you over to my bed. I sit right beside you, so close our legs touch, babbling on and on about how I will be the mommy and you will be the daddy and my dolls will be our babies. It's not long before you say it's boring, and ask if I want to play with a real baby instead, and be a real family. I tell you that it is just a game, just pretend, that I'm not a real mommy. But you promise that you know a way to make me a real mommy, and that you can show me, if I want. You tell me not to be scared, and that you will try not to hurt me, then you push my shoulders down onto the barney sheets and pull my feet into your lap. I giggle as you tickle my toes, then my legs, then your hands slip under my big bird nightgown. You are touching my underwear, and sliding them down my legs. I sit up, asking what you are doing. You tell me to trust you, and push me back on the bed. Then you are touching me, and I am pulling away. You tell me I need to stay still as you crawl on top of me. I tell you that it hurts, and keep trying to close my legs, but you hold them open. I start crying when you start getting mad. You say I am too small. That you thought I was a big girl but I was really just a baby. I tell you I'm not a baby and you say, "Prove it." You finish in my mouth and tell me I have to swallow. Then you put my underwear back on, tuck me in bed, and leave, closing the door behind you.

Chapter 3

I was a preschooler that wanted to be dead.

I don't think I consciously knew what was going on was a bad thing, but I think deep down part of me did. I felt dirty and used, and I didn't know what to do with these feelings. I didn't want to be alive anymore.

I tried to kill myself, when I was four. My parents were watching a movie when they thought I was in bed. I secretly sat on the stairs watching. In the movie, a man got hung. Which gave me the ever so brilliant idea.

I don't remember if I knew the man died. I don't remember if I knew it could kill me. I don't remember what I thought would happen. I do remember feeling so dirty that I didn't want to be me anymore. I don't think I was necessarily trying to kill myself, though I don't know what else I would have been trying to achieve. I just know that I wanted everything to stop.

I pulled the red picnic table over to the tree that had a rope on it. It was a blue and white rope that I would swing on, pretending to be Tarzan. This time though, I was playing a much more serious game. I tied it around my neck and stood on the edge of the picnic table.

I don't remember what I was thinking in that moment. All I remember is stepping off the table, and not being able to breathe. I felt my legs kicking. I saw my brother come around the corner of the garage, right before my eyes rolled back in my head. Then I don't remember anything.

I don't know why my brother didn't tell my parents. Then again, how would he tell them that their four-year-old tried to kill herself? Plus, I shouldn't be the one talking, I mean, why didn't I tell? About anything? Why did I keep it all a secret for fourteen years?

Things were so complicated. The thought of telling someone was nonexistent for a long time. Why would I tell someone when I didn't know it was wrong? And when I did finally realize it was wrong I was addicted to the attention, and some part of me just knew that if I told, he wouldn't want to be my friend anymore. That's what he was to me, my friend. I didn't know then that friends don't do the things he did. Friends don't take advantage of weaknesses and exploit trust. Friends don't have sex with little kids.

Chapter 4

I was a child that didn't know how to say no.

So things continued. Whenever he decided to stop over, and every Sunday after church. But they didn't have to. When I was six I could have been saved. Years of abuse could have been ended in a moment. It all came down to the one man who failed me.

I'm six. It's after church, and I'm helping you clean up. We are in the sacristy putting everything away. The servers and lectors are still coming in and out, but gradually people come in less and less frequently.

Eventually your fingers begin playing with my shirt. Then the top of my skirt. You take the chalice I'm holding out of my hands and set it aside. You push everything on the counter out of the way, lift me up, and set me down. You slide my long, silky purple skirt up over my thighs and run your fingers across my legs. "Do you want to play a game?" You ask. I shake my head and you frown. The air freezes in my lungs and my muscles lock into place. "You sure?" You ask, tucking my hair behind my ear. I just stare at you, then hop off the counter.

I pick up the chalice again, as you play with my hair and start telling me how much you love me. How beautiful I am. You start kissing my neck. Then someone clears his throat. You jump away from me like you just got burned. The priest stands behind us. No one says anything. Then you recompose yourself, walk over and whisper with him. He looks up and makes eye contact with me, nods, and walks out. He leaves me. You shut the door behind him and lock it, then turn to me. Your hands are shaking. They wrap around my neck as you tell me not to cry.

I didn't know what to think. In the moment when the priest walked in I was terrified. I felt like I had been caught doing something terrible. But when he left I felt so abandoned. Did he not realize what he was leaving me with? That was the day I stopped trusting people.

Chapter 5

I was a kindergartener that was brainwashed.

I began to hate myself. Not surprising considering what was happening to me. When I was six I thought I was fat. I worried about the bulge in my stomach and how my thighs touched. I believed my face was chubby and I thought I was the ugliest person on the planet. My eyes were too far apart. My nose was too big. It didn't matter how many people stopped my mother in the grocery store to tell her how pretty I was, or gasp at my eyes. I started to hate everything about myself, how I looked, how I talked. It didn't matter. If there was any association to myself, I hated it.

There is obviously a problem when a six year old thinks about dying. I thought about killing myself often. I don't think I really wanted to die. I just wanted to make it stop. I wanted to get away from it all. I felt so dirty and bad. I knew what we did was wrong. Some part of me just knew it wasn't supposed to be happening, but I still never told. I just found ways to deal with it myself.

That was the first time I cut myself, when I was six. One day I realized how sharp the scissors were, and I wondered what would happen if I dragged them across my skin. So I set the scissors against my skin and pressed down. I watched the little beads of blood form in the line where the skin separated. And I panicked. I couldn't believe that I had done that. I ran inside and told my mom that the cat scratched me. Mommy cleaned my arm and put a band-aid on. Everything was all better. Except it wasn't.

That night I thought long and hard about what I had done. I didn't realize what it was I was feeling at the time. But now I recognize it. I was feeling power. It was an emotion so foreign to me that I didn't even have a name for it. I had spent so long completely powerless that having the opposite feeling terrified me. I was scared of what I was capable of doing. I realized that I wanted to do it again, but I was too afraid to attempt the act another time. It would be years before this behavior would surface again.

Chapter 6

I was a living dead girl.

It continued this way for a few years. There was abuse after church every week. But it was bearable. Then things changed. When I was seven it stopped being just my abuser that had sex with me. He started to sell me. I don't know who the men were. I don't know where I was at. I really don't know much at all. But what I do know is that it happened.

I heard an unfamiliar voice say, "Let me have a turn with her."

Then I hear you say, "No, she's mine."

He counters with, "I'll pay you."

To which you reply, "How much?" Then I don't hear anything. Just some shuffling and bumping around. I prayed you weren't talking about me. But prayer was always a waste of breath. The door opened and you said, "Fifteen minutes." Then it closed again. I could feel him standing there. I heard the clanks of metal and a zipper. Then a thump as his pants and belt fell to the floor. The bed sank on one side as he sat. I felt cold air hit my back as the sheets were peeled back. I could feel him sliding closer, then his rough hands rubbing across my skin. Damp, hot breath assaulted my neck. I felt him getting hard as he crawled on top of me. Kissing my neck, fingers twining in my hair, weight stealing the air from my lungs, trapping me beneath him. Humid air in my ear. A warning; relax. Then pain.

I don't know much about that day. I don't know where I was. I don't know who it was. I do know that I didn't scream. I don't know why.

I worked in a preschool for a few years when I was older. Hearing kids fight over toys saying, "Let me have a turn!" and in reply, "No! It's mine!" sent me back to this moment. Back to the feelings of powerlessness and betrayal. Feelings of fear and disgust. But mostly betrayal.

How could he do this to me? The sex made sense when it was with him, he loved me. But with other men? There was no explanation. It made no sense. I was so confused that I didn't even try to stop it. I rationalized it away thinking, "Maybe everyone does this." Plus by then, the threats were beginning.

Chapter 7

I was a scared little girl.

People ask me why I didn't tell. But that question is much more easily asked than answered. I guess I have a few explanations. It started so young that for a long time I didn't realize it was wrong. I hated what was happening, but I didn't know it was anything that I needed to tell anyone. It was just an accident, or a game. Even when parts of me began to have a feeling that it was wrong, I didn't have the words to tell anyone what was happening.

When I did finally realize what was going on was not supposed to be, things were a little more complicated. He was my friend. Practically my dad. I looked up to him and went to him for advice. He knew my favorite things and the names of my friends. He knew everything about me. He would hug me and love me. I trusted him. I knew that if I ever told I would lose him. Even though that's what part of me wanted, the majority of me needed him in my life.

A huge piece that stopped me from telling was the realization that it was my fault. I thought that I had to have done something for him to pick me over the millions of the children all around the world. It had to be my fault because there was no one else to blame.

And most complicated of all, I loved him. I was utterly infatuated by him. I was the princess and he was my knight in shining armor. He promised to marry me, and I believed him. I loved the attention he gave me and the compliments he showered me with. I loved everything about him. I was afraid to tell because I knew it would make him hate me. He told me how the cops would take me away and I would never see him again, and that terrified me.

    The moment when the priest walked in, and I thought I had gotten freedom, my heart felt so light. But later, the idea of having my freedom was enough to send me running straight back into the arms of my abuser.

Chapter 8

I was so confused.

I was nine when I decided I was done. I was sick of all the sex and wanted it to stop. But he suddenly changed. He went from my knight in shining armor to a monster I never knew existed. I had no idea what I was up against. I thought that I could handle it myself. I was wrong.

"I don't want to do this anymore." You look at me for a long time. Narrow your eyes. I can tell you are thinking hard about what to say next. Searching for the right reaction.

"What do you mean, you don't want to do this anymore?"

"All this. I'm done. I want it to stop." You're not even looking at me anymore. Don't even bother.

"Jessica, you really think you have a choice? You don't get to decide when it stops. I do. I own you. You were put on this Earth for my pleasure. That's it. That is your purpose in life. You belong to me." I stare at you, not comprehending. You've been nothing but kind to me my entire life. I have no idea how to react to this sudden change of character.

"Why are you being so mean to me?" I ask you. You finally look at me again. Slowly, you answer.

"I'm not being mean, I'm being honest. Everyone else lies to you. They say they love you, but they don't. They really hate you, your parents, and friends. I'm the only one who really loves you."

"You're lying." Tears are pooling in my eyes. You give me a sad smile and put your hands on my shoulders.

"Have I ever lied to you?"

    I thought for such a long time after this conversation. He was right. He had never lied to me before. I knew he loved me, maybe he was right about everyone else hating me. Maybe he was the only one that would ever love me. Now I realize this was total bullshit. It was only another manipulation tactic he used to get me to feel isolated from the rest of the world. A way to make me utterly dependent on him. It worked.

Chapter 9

I was a girl in a plaid uniform.

He became mean. But I thought it was something I had done to make him change. I began to hate him, but I still needed him. It was so complicated I didn't even know what I was feeling most of the time. I continued to believe that I loved him. He was going to marry me, remember? The way I saw it, married people fight, maybe they hate each other sometimes too. I rationalized everything he did to me, but little by little he pushed me to my breaking point.

I went to him again and told him I was done, that I was telling. He just shook his head and said, "we already had this conversation." And that was that. End of discussion.

    I think he started drugging me. Things got weird then. Memories are all hazy and mixed-up. Know those fun house mirrors that distort everything? That's what the memories of this time are like, distorted. Everything comes and goes. I remember some things crystal clear, like the bedding that my hands wrapped around, or the jeans laying on the floor. But I don't remember the important things, like faces or locations, much to the frustration of the detectives and attorneys later on.

    That's only the things I remember. There is so much I don't. I remember a few times of pretending to be normal at school, and a couple times I got in trouble at home for dumb stuff like getting paint in the carpet of my room. But other than that, these couple years are just a jumbled up blur that I can't sort into distinct memories. That part of my life might as well be gone. I might be better off if it was.

Chapter 10

I was a girl that gave in.

I stopped fighting when I was 12.

"You're beautiful you know."

I glance up, then drop my eyes. "No I'm not." You smile, and lean in closer. Close enough that I can see each eyelash when my eyes dart up to see your reaction.

"Yes you are." You tuck my hair behind my ear, and I know what you want. But I don't want to do this. I'm sick of this game of yours.

"This isn't right." I mumble.

"So what?"

"We can't do this anymore." *I'm breathing fast. My voice is tight. "Why are you doing this?"*

"Because I like you, and you like me. It makes sense." Your hand curls around my neck and pulls me in for a kiss. But I pull away.

"I have to-"

"Not yet." You pull me in again. Tears start sliding down my face. You stop and sigh. Then hug me. I melt in your arms. You feel safe. But then it's over. You push me onto my back. "You're beautiful" you say again, as your face comes above mine. I give up. Why fight something I deserve?

When I stopped fighting, I also stopped eating. I dealt with my abuser by not dealing with him. I let him do whatever he wanted, then I coped with what he did by starving myself. When I was alone, I wouldn't eat a bite. In public though, I ate like normal, to keep up the perfect daughter facade. That was when I still had control.

It didn't take long for that to leave though. Soon I was left with nothing but an illusion of control. I thought I could handle starving myself, and soon enough, exercising like crazy, but I couldn't.

I'd seen those girls that had eating disorders. I knew there were people out there who starved themselves until they died, but never once did the thought cross my mind that I could be one of them. Never once did I think I would ever gain the title of "anorexic." But I did.

It started so innocent, like everything does. Going on a diet. But that diet turned into skipping a meal, and then two. That diet became lying about eating and exercising until I passed out. That diet became a constant frozen feeling, and an ever present ache in my stomach. A loss of hair and of happiness. A complete loss of control and any slight resemblance of normal my life consisted of. That diet became my life.

Chapter 11

I was in a mental prison.

People started to notice. It looks suspicious when a 13 year old girl starts skipping lunch every day. When a little girl runs more than she talks. People started wondering, especially when my skin became pale and my cheeks sunken in. I became fragile, breakable. I curled in on myself and jumped at the slightest noise or touch. But I insisted that I was fine. I lied to everyone and used my "lawyer skills" to manipulate them all into thinking I was okay. But they only backed off for so long.

I stopped eating in front of people as well. I would find excuses to constantly skip meals, and only pick at my food when I actually attended. The weight just kept sliding off. And I loved it. I felt like I was in control for once in my life. There was so much abuse happening that I had no say in. Food, or rather, lack of food, became my source of power. Starving myself felt good. I felt right for once in my life. I didn't deserve the food to begin with, because I was a bad person. Starving myself made me wither away little by little, until I would finally disappear and never be in the way again. I wouldn't be a waste of space anymore. Plus, princesses are skinny.

Now I see how sick I was, but at the time, it felt so true. People starting telling me how concerned they were. I was constantly in the guidance counselor's office. Even my principal talked to me. Teachers would walk me to lunch. Friends would report me for not eating.

My parents made me see a therapist, Franne. I hated her. (In the beginning at least.) I would go each week and sit there, staring at her without speaking. She tried her hardest, but there is only so much that can be done when someone is so reluctant. Some weeks I just wouldn't go, and my principal would come pull me from class and send me to Franne's office. And I would sit there, and stare, or more accurately, glare.

I didn't talk because I knew that the moment I started talking, I wouldn't be able to stop. And I would spill every secret my heart was holding. That was something that just couldn't happen. Everything would fall apart if that happened.

And though it was all supposed to be helping me, it only felt like the little pieces of control I had remaining were beginning to slip through my fingers.

Chapter 12

I was a girl that trusted too much.

Everything was falling apart. The little bits of control that I thought I had were crumbling between my fingers. The abuse was getting worse and worse the longer it continued.

You are telling me to take my clothes off, but I don't want to, and I refuse. You tell me I'm so beautiful, you just need to see my body. But I'm not convinced, and I shake my head and stare at the ground. He kinda chuckles as he says, "I don't care about consent" and grabs my upper arm and a handful of my shirt. I slap him. He almost hits me back, but you take me in your arms, saying something about not leaving a bruise. You pull me to your chest, telling me to breathe, relax, I'm safe. You will never let anything hurt me. You tell me to listen to your heart, because I'm the only reason it keeps beating.

We stand like that for a long time, my ear pressed to your chest, your arms around me. Then you tilt my chin up and gently kiss me. You don't even use your tongue, because you know I don't like it. I think it's one of the sweetest kisses we ever have. Then the hand you have on my chin moves to the back of my neck and the hand on my back pushes up a piece of my shirt as you rub your thumb across my back. Suddenly in one smooth motion, my shirt is off.

I cross my arms immediately and duck my head, feeling pathetic and ashamed. You try to hug me again but I don't let you. You grab at my arms and I push you away. You say my name, all soft and sad. Saying how this is all just a part of life, and the sooner I learn to deal with it, the better. Your hand snares my wrist, and his arms wrap around me from behind. His lips suction onto my neck and I let my legs go numb, thinking he will drop me. But he doesn't. His hands float across my chest. You turn me around and let go of my wrist as he pulls me to his body.

 You are watching from a few feet away with a camera. I push against his chest and turn my head away. One arm holds me to him, the other slides down my stomach and into my pants. I lose it, hitting and kicking. You are back then, trying to restrain me. I'm in the air for a second, but my wild flailing causes you to drop me. I dart for the door but someone's hands grab my hips and pull me back. You get me on my back and grab the waist of my pants, pulling them down my legs while I kick at anything in reach. You gesture towards me and say, "All yours." You pick up the camera again as he lays on top of me. I claw at him as he swears.

You swoop in to save the day, clamping metal around my wrist. Both arms are pulled roughly above my head, there is a click and you both relax. I yank at my arms, but they are handcuffed around a pole. He unbuttons his pants as I kick and twist on the floor. He pulls my legs apart as his face replaces them. I strain against everything; his mouth on my skin, your hands on my mouth, my arms above my head. I do everything I can to get away from him as he enters me. But it's no use. I can't breathe. The air refuses to fill my lungs. Each gasp makes them ache.

Finally, laying there naked, I give up. I'm not there anymore. I focus on a dent in the wall that just becomes a blurry shape as tears leak down my face. Someone else has a turn, and another, and who knows how many others. I get passed around like a joint, everybody taking a turn. I don't know where my mind goes, but it isn't in my body. I just focus on my dent in the wall.

Somewhere in that time, I think I might be dying, and I really wish it was true.

Chapter 13

I was a child without safety.

I made it stop. The abuse. I stopped it for a few months. I made myself invisible, a ghost. I made it so he could never get access to me. I spent as much time as possible at school and activities. Whenever I was home alone, I would leave all the lights off and make it seem like no one was there. When he came over I wouldn't leave the family. Not even to use the restroom. I left the second church was over. He would follow me out, and call my name. But I kept walking, sometimes even running to get away. And it worked, for a while. I was on a run when he found me, and kidnapped me. I was only fourteen.

It is the middle or end of November. The sky is white and gray, like it could dump buckets of snow or rain and any second. I am in a gray track sweatshirt and leggings. I don't have any socks on. Mom and I had gotten a fight over something stupid and pointless and I'd stormed out of the house. Of course I didn't want to go back and get my socks because that would hurt my pride, so I was without.

I am about five miles from home and I am regretting it. Blisters are forming on my feet, so I start to walk. Everything is still; the air, the birds, everything. I am breathing so hard and so deep in my head that I don't hear you come. But then your car is beside me and you are offering me a ride.

I try to sound firm as I say no. I want you to know I'm not scared. You laugh but you look pissed. You suggest I get in and I decline. You kind of squint at me then pull ahead and pull over. My stomach flips. You get out and casually walked over to me, put your arm across my shoulders and start saying how we haven't talked in awhile and that makes you sad. I say something about getting home and shrug your arm off. You grab my arm. It's a warning, a "don't test me" type of thing. I look up at you and you smile, "how about that ride?"

    I still don't really know how I get in the car. But I do. You are talking about my old obsession with princesses and how you are my knight in shining armor. You always said you would protect me and make sure no one ever hurt me. You claim you always waited for the day I needed you so you could come save me. Like you just had. Because you love me so much and would do anything for me. You put your hand on my knee and squeeze. It stays there for a while but then it starts gliding up. I tense, and you tell me to relax. I push your hand off. You put it back and I shove it off again. I pull my legs to my chest and you smirk, and put your hand on my knee again.

Eventually we get to your farm. You get out of the car and I know I'm expected to follow. What choice do I have? We are in the middle of nowhere. I am miles from home. I drag my feet behind you as you hold the door open for me. I hesitate and you raise an eyebrow, so I walk in. There is a click and I realize you locked the door behind us. I feel the walls collapsing around me and I can't breathe. You take a step towards me and I throw up. You call me a fat-ass, and storm off, then throw paper towels in the room. You watch me bend over to clean it up and start talking, saying how you missed me, and how long you been waiting for this. You start saying all the things you are going to do to me. I run into the bathroom. The doorknob rattles. You start punching and kicking the door. My legs give out so I curl up in the corner. You scream every name you can think of. Then everything goes quiet.

Here is a missing chunk. I don't know how I get out of the bathroom. The next thing I remember is sitting on the couch. Every muscle is as tight as it can possibly go. You pull my hair out of the ponytail and start smoothing it out, tucking it behind my ears. You lean in and I turn. I say I don't want to. You try to make me face you. When I won't, you start kissing my neck. I try getting up but your arms are like metal. I start pushing at you and moving my head trying to get you to stop. Which is exactly what you want.

You crush your lips to mine and I push against your chest, but you barely even notice. You push me down into the couch as I say, "no. I don't want to." You crawl on top of me and respond, "I didn't ask." I am pinned beneath you as your fingers knot in my hair and your tongue forces its way into my mouth. I feel your hand start sliding underneath my shirt, and I begin hitting and kicking. I feel you starting to get hard, and I punch you. Immediately, your hands wrap around my neck and you shake me, telling me to stop being such a bitch.

    You rip my sweatshirt off, and I am laying there in my bra while you straddle me. You lean back, and I realize you are enjoying this. Slowly, my bra comes off, and I just lay there, frozen, afraid fighting back will cause you to choke me again. Your hands and face go to my chest, and I remain a statue, until your fingers slip under the elastic of my leggings. I strike at your face, and you rip my pants off, shoes along with them. You keep kissing me as your fingers massage me. I start thrashing and you warn me that it's only going to hurt more as you tear my underwear down to my knees.

    I'm completely naked. I punch and kick. Your hands fly up to my throat and my head flies back into the arm of the couch, loud enough there is a resounding crack. My eyes fill with tears. You stop, lay your head down on my chest, apologizing as you stroke my stomach. You say you're sorry, and didn't mean to hurt me, how you never want to hurt me. You just love me so much, you can't help yourself sometimes. But it's ok, because this is what people do when they're in love.

You lean back then, and unbuckle your pants. I start crying. I tell you I don't want to, I promise not to tell anyone if you just stop now. You cover my mouth and start rubbing yourself against my stomach, promising it will be over soon. I'm crying so hard I can hardly speak as I beg you not to. But you don't care, and thrust into me anyway. I have never felt pain so intense before. I scream, but no one is around to hear me. You do it again, and again.

I go limp. There is nothing I can do to stop you. I just close my eyes and wait for it to be over. I don't feel or hear anything anymore. Time no longer exists. It could be minutes, or hours, I wouldn't know the difference. I might as well be dead. I wish I was. Eventually you get off me. But you aren't done. Not much later you pull me into the kitchen and do it again. Then we go to the couch one more time. When you're finished you throw my clothes at me and tell me to get dressed. Then you drive me home. Before I get out of the car I ask, "How could you."

You barely even glance at me when you reply, "Oh don't play the victim. You wanted it. If you didn't you would have fought harder. You were practically begging for it, filthy slut."

Chapter 14

I was a girl that broke apart.

My crown fell off. My castle crumbled. I broke. I was done. I no longer wanted to be alive. So I made a plan.

I was going to kill myself. I didn't really want to die but I had no other choice. There was nothing else I could do. I had it all set up and ready to go. But there was one flaw in my plan; I talked to the guidance counselor. After all the time she had invested, I felt like I at least needed to thank her for putting up with me. Somehow, she knew what I was doing. Depression is a symptom of anorexia, maybe she saw it coming.

My mother was called and warned. Before school was out that day I received a note telling me to go to her office after school. When I arrived she was crying. She told me she couldn't bear to lose me, and that she didn't know I was in so much pain.

We went to the ER, where I was admitted to the Psych Ward. I sat in my room that night looking for all the ways I could possibly kill myself. There were very few, and even the ideas I had were long shots. I could slam my head against the wall until I died, but they would come in too soon. I could break a light and slit my wrists, but they would stop me before I would bleed out. My options were limited.

The next morning a lady sat across from me asking me questions. "Why do you want to kill yourself?" I just shrugged and looked out the window. What was I supposed to say? *I don't know why I want to be dead, oh, wait, I'm being abused, and I have been for as long as I can remember. I feel dirty and used and I just want it to stop.* Ya right. Not happening. So I just stayed quiet. Not really the response they were looking for.

Chapter 15

I was a confused, conflicted teen.

They sent me to a behavioral health center. There I met a group of teenagers with issues like self-harm, suicide attempts, etc. I was in a whole different world. Again, I coped by not eating, but apparently, starving yourself was not look highly upon. Most of my time there was spent sitting at a table with a shake supplement in front of me while everyone else was in group. If I refused it, I was put on bed rest, which is not nearly as fun as one might assume. And I realized that at the rate I was going, I was never going to get out.

I started to play the game. I discovered ways to make my food disappear, and not into my stomach. I figured out how to see the scale when they weighed me backwards every morning. I learned how to hide things in my gown so the scale would show a stable weight. I took all their tests and swallowed their pills. I answered all their questions and followed the system. Essentially, I played them, and it was surprisingly easy.

"How long have you been sad?" My answer? A long time. Not a lie.

"Why do you want to kill yourself?" Response for this one? Something about school and stress. Totally bullshit. Not like I would tell them that though. They nodded and wrote stupid observations on their stupid notepads.

"What are some things you can do when you feel this way again?" Notice they said when, not if, like I'm guaranteed to feel this shitty again. I replied with the first things that popped into my head. Art, music, friends. They smiled and nodded and wrote my new "coping skills" down.

"Who are some people you can go to when you feel bad?" Notice, they said when again. I rattled off a few names, rolling my eyes when they weren't looking. Like I would ever call anyone. My logic? If I wanted to kill myself I would, I wasn't going to call someone up to tell them first. But my answers and new behaviors were satisfactory.

A normal stay was 5-7 days. I stayed for 13. I was discharged with a diagnosis of depression, anxiety, and an eating disorder. They encouraged further specialized treatment for my eating disorder, but I assured my parents I was fine, and I was taken home, and back to Franne's office.

Chapter 16

I was a girl that fought every battle.

I think Franne expected me to be over my silent glaring phase. I wasn't. I still passed hours in her office with my arms crossed and a frown on my face.

I think everyone expected me to be better. I wasn't. Starving myself made me feel powerful. I finally felt like I had some control. When I didn't eat, I was strong. I was beautiful. At least I thought so. He didn't agree. He transformed into the concerned parent, telling me I needed to.take care of myself. Part of me thought, "maybe if I get skinny enough he'll be so concerned he stops everything just to take care of me." It was a stupid thought. He didn't care. In fact, he liked it, I didn't have any boobs. I still looked like a kid. The only downside was that my bones stabbed him during sex.

Why would I give up starving myself? I just got better at hiding it. People were watching me eat. But I counted every calorie and started exercising. Every day after school every calorie I ate would be burned off, and I wouldn't stop until I reached a net amount of zero. Most days, I even exercised more than I would eat. I started skipping lunch again, hiding in the chapel. But it could only last so long. I had lost control. My principal found me skipping lunch. I'm sure my mother was called again and again. Finally they had enough.

They told me I was going to treatment. This time it was a longer term situation, specifically for my eating disorder. I went on a rampage. Did they really think I wanted help? I tore my room apart and packed a bag, saying I was running away. My parents just told me to be ready because we were leaving in two days. I didn't run away. It was the middle of winter and I was 14. I wasn't entirely stupid. Two days later I ended up in a car with a suitcase packed, on my way to an inpatient hospital for eating disorders.

Chapter 17

I was an anorexic that didn't want to get better.

The last thing I wanted to do was eat. But I was on a locked unit for severe eating disorders. Not eating wasn't really an option. I thought it was. I guess I figured that if I fought it long enough the hospital would give up and get rid of me. Newsflash! It doesn't work that way.

I was much worse than I thought I was. The doctors were concerned about cardiac arrest. I had a heart monitor on full time, and an I.V. port put in my hand so medicine could be administered quickly if my heart was to stop. I still thought it was all a game.

I woke up each morning to eat breakfast, a huge breakfast, meant for little girls that need to gain major weight. Then sat in what was called "observation" for an hour. Observation was basically just all the patients not being allowed to go out of the main room so the nurses can ensure no one is purging. Then we had snack, and observation. Then lunch, and observation. Snack again, and observation. Now dinner, and observation. Finally snack, and observation. Throw in a couple groups and therapy sessions, and that was life on the unit.

He told me he would write to me, and he did. He sent vulgar letters, along with presents of rosaries and holy water. The ultimate contradiction. I don't know if he actually cared, or was just missing his fuck toy. Either way, I ripped his letters up and threw everything away. Sometimes I didn't even bother to open his presents. They went straight from the hands of the nurse to the mouth of the trash.

The doctors didn't think my plan of being so annoying and resistant that they would give up on me was a good idea. They began to threaten me with the idea of a feeding tube. They explained how it would go up my nose and down into my stomach. Not thinking of the logistics, this didn't seem like too big a deal. So I figured, whatever, and kept doing the same things I had been doing. Guess what I ended up getting?

The first time I got a feeding tube I didn't fight it. I should have. It was one of the most uncomfortable things I've ever experienced. The tube has a metal wire in it when they force it up the nose and down the throat. Tears filled my eyes as they told me to swallow while I gasped to get enough air in my lungs.

The hurt didn't go away. It hurt to sleep. It hurt to swallow. It hurt each time I put my hair behind my ear and accidentally tugged on the tube. It hurt when they squeezed calories through my feeding tube, though that one might have just been in my mind. So I did the only thing I could think of, I pulled the tube out.

I remember they didn't notice immediately. I had a nurse talk to me, I just acted normal and she left me alone. A few minutes later she came back, realizing what was different about me. She looked in the garbage, saw the devil tube, and shook her head, commenting on how the doctor was not going to be amused. I didn't really care. Until they tried to put another tube in.

Four people tried to hold me down. For being a pile of bones, I was quite strong. They brought in two more people. I fought with everything I had in me. Somehow I got myself to the floor, where logically I crawled under the bed so they couldn't get me. The psychiatrist was not amused. She sat in my room for an hour trying to rationalize with me. I used my highly evolved manipulation skills, and we negotiated. The feeding tube would stay out, but I couldn't skip any more food. She must have known she was setting me up for failure, but I thought it was a good deal. It's not like I was actually planning on eating anyways.

I got smarter. I found ways to hide food. I took as long a shower as possible and exercised like a madman while the water cascaded around me. But my "eating" couldn't last. I got in an argument with one of the staff, and ended up refusing to drink the leftover juice from my fruit cup. Rationalizing the amount of calories remaining in the juice, and the amount in the supplement, I refused that as well. And got another feeding tube, which I promptly removed. Again.

Chapter 18

I was a teen they called a liar.

They tried to give me another feeding tube. But this time I was ready for it. Two security guards and six nurses later they had had enough. They pulled my pants down and gave me a shot in the butt. I don't know if it was the fact that I was being restrained, or the fact that my pants got pulled down, but I had the first flashback of my life.

I was terrified. I didn't know what was happening. I thought the abuse was over, but here I was, feeling like I was living it again. I hit and kicked and screamed, for a different reason than they thought. But no one knew what was happening.

Once again, I felt like a complete piece of shit. I was dirty and worthless all over again. When they left me I dug in my box of colored pencils and found my pencil sharpener. I stuck my fingernail in the rivets of the screw and twisted. Out fell the blade. For the second time in my life I pressed a blade against my skin and pushed down. And finally I felt relief.

Until the nightmares began. I would wake up screaming with the bed soaked in cold sweat. So I stopped sleeping. I slept on average maybe two hours a night. I kept myself awake as long as possible, until I finally crashed from complete exhaustion. I went into a hyperactive state, and basically had more energy to compensate for my lack of sleep.

I didn't last very long like this. Finally I went to my therapist. I showed her my cuts. And I told her about the flashback. It took all my strength to finally tell someone what had happened to me. I was curled up in a ball on the floor in her office when I told. I tried to tell her about the time I was kidnapped. She wanted a name, but I couldn't give it to her. I could tell that she didn't know how to reply to me. She was a young therapist, this was probably her first job out of college. So she went to the rest of the team. Guess what they decided? I was making it all up for attention. They told my parents, and dropped it. They never even told the police. I was a terrified 14 year old girl, finally trying to tell my secret, and they told me to stop lying.

Chapter 19

I was a little girl trying to be a hero.

Eventually I got out of there. Good riddance. I went home, and decided that he was never going to touch me again. I told my parents he made me uncomfortable, and they told him not to talk to me. He defied their orders, following me out of church and bringing me presents. We stopped going to church there. Eventually, we moved. Goodbye small town and hello to the slightly bigger town about 10 miles away. And that was the end of that phase of my life, or so I thought. But it didn't go away. One day, I slit my arm from wrist to elbow, and ended up at the psych ward again. I didn't want to be alive. That year I went to school with my arm wrapped up, coming up with elaborate stories to explain how it got that way.

Somewhere along the way, I stopped hating Franne. To be honest, I began to love her. Franne's office became my safe space, and Franne was my safe person. I told her when I self-harmed and when I sexted. I told her everything. Literally everything. She was the first and only person I was ever so open and honest with. I think that's where the most healing took place. Sure, there were times when I hated her, and yelled at her when she pushed the wrong buttons, but everything she did was out of love. When I first started seeing her, after the silent phase, I told her she would abandon me when she found out how fucked-up I was. Franne promised she would always stay by my side, and she always has, even through some horrible times.

I don't remember how I found out, but I learned he was grooming another little girl. I went to my guidance counselor, and we went to the police together. I was terrified. I went into one of those little interrogation rooms like on TV. The detective asked me a bunch of questions, and halfway through the interview I changed my mind. I told him I made it all up. When he asked why I would make this up I replied with what had been told to me; for attention.

    I started to have a lot of sex. With random men. It was my way to get back at my abuser, to me, it was cheating. I wanted to hurt him for hurting me. I had sex with men twice my age and sexted men even older. It was my way to find validation and what felt like love. I felt horrible for what I was doing, but I didn't know what else to do. Sex also gave me control. After years of helplessness I had finally found a way to feel empowered. I wasn't forced to do anything. I was completely in control.

After that, an older friend took me to see an advocate at Safe Harbor. I sat there with my head down shaking my leg the entire time. The advocate gave me her card, completely sure I would never step foot back in her office. But for some reason, eventually I went back on my own. She came with me when I went to a child advocacy center. I told them my secrets, but halfway through, I panicked. I realized I was betraying him, and I told them I was done. But it was too late.

I tortured myself thinking things like, "Maybe I'm just overreacting. Maybe none of the abuse was even that bad. I'm probably just exaggerating. He is a good person, am I really going to ruin his life?"

I spent every waking hour torturing myself. I couldn't focus in school, or doing homework. I started to fail tests, something I had never done in my life. Even worse, I didn't care. I stopped eating, and began self-harming anew. Sleeping was practically impossible. My thoughts began screaming at night, and when exhaustion took over, the nightmares began. But I had already made my choice to tell.

An investigation was started. They took my journals and all the presents he had given me. They took the letters he had written me, and it all went to the grand jury, where I had to testify. That same day, my abuser was arrested. He spent 33 days in jail. I counted. He was charged with 16 crimes including sexual contact with a minor, rape, and aggravated kidnapping. His bond was set at one million dollars. Then it got dropped to 500,000. Then 300,000. He only had to pay 30,000 to get out, which he did.

Chapter 20

I was a girl trying to free herself.

I was terrified. I recanted my entire story. Then un-recanted. I was so conflicted. They told me I had Stockholm Syndrome. I didn't want anything bad to happen to him, I loved him. I was his princess. But I was terrified he would come at me, to retaliate for what I put him through. I couldn't imagine how horrible jail must have been. I was sure he would come and hurt me. But I was his princess.

I didn't want him doing the same things he did to me to another little girl. I went to the child advocacy center again. This time I told them almost everything. I started going in to talk to the state's attorney. I honestly, really wanted to help however I could, but I still wasn't committed. I lied about what I remembered, trying to hide certain things he did.

My mood changed with the day. One day I would be so willing to help, giving any details I could remember. Other days I would freak out about helping to put him in jail, and I would claim everything was made up. I honestly wasn't trying to be so manipulative, I was just so confused. I didn't know what I wanted, and I was so afraid. It was all so complicated. My head kept going back and forth between denial and outrage. The internal dialogue went something like this:

"I love him and he loves me. No he didn't. Whatever they thought was going on with the girl, it had to be a mistake. No, you knew he would do this. No, he would never. Yes he would. He loved me. Not enough. They got it all wrong. He was going to do it to her. No, I was special. Apparently not. He just made a mistake. All he does is make mistakes. It doesn't mean he meant to hurt her. You have to tell. I can't. You must. He never meant to hurt anyone. Count the times he hurt you. He's not a bad person. But would a good person do the things he did? He didn't mean to. You're telling."

And then, "I shouldn't have told. You did the right thing. I'm ruining his life. He ruined yours. He didn't mean to. We've been through this. I'm going to tell them I lied. That will ruin everything. I already ruined everything. He needs to be in jail to protect kids. If he has me he doesn't need to hurt anyone. Newsflash, you're not with him. I'm going to tell everyone I lied and go back to him. They won't believe you or let you. Too late, I told them. They don't believe you. So what? They know you're lying. I'm trying as hard as I can. Tell them you lied about lying. I can't.

Back and forth my brain went. There were two sides battling each other day and night. Sometimes they would agree, or one side would win, and I would make decisions I would regret later, like telling, or saying I made everything up. It frustrated everyone, but they just didn't understand how confusing this was for me. They tried to understand, but they just couldn't.

They weren't stupid. They caught onto my games and told me that the case was going to fall apart. Someone told me that I was going to get eaten alive on the stand. But there were things I couldn't tell them. I felt that certain parts of my story belonged just to me. I was afraid they would judge me and think I was as disgusting as I felt. I didn't want to see the pity in their eyes when they realized how fucked-up I was. I got scared. I realized that I couldn't testify. So I drank a bottle of Nyquil. And was sent to treatment number two.

This time I was in treatment in Arizona for trauma and an eating disorder. I was 16 now. I hated it there. The staff was power-tripping and made rules just because they could. They didn't care about any of the patients at all. I think they hated me too, I pointed out all the flaws in the system. At one point I even called patient advocacy to talk about the rights we had as patients that were being violated. Only problem with that was the guy I called actually worked for the guy I was complaining about. So that got nowhere.

Eventually I had enough. I convinced a group of girls to run away with me. Five of us altogether took off running one night. I hitchhiked on the busiest road in the U.S. The stretch of road between Vegas and Phoenix. On Super bowl Sunday, which was in Phoenix. Plus it was coyote season. Not my brightest idea.

Long, long story short, we ended up back at the treatment facility in some deep shit. I was the "ringleader" and the treatment center was done with me. They tried to send me off to a boarding school. The day I found out is the day I ran for the second time. It was my 17th birthday. My golden birthday. It wasn't very golden. I didn't get very far before I had an asthma attack. They found me laying in the desert. They called the police, and I ended up in the E.R.

Chapter 21

I was a teenager in major trouble.

The boarding school I was supposed to go to wouldn't take me anymore because I was a flight risk. So my parents found a wilderness camp. Before I left the hospital I said the most cruel things to my parents. I told them they were horrible parents, they didn't protect me. They hadn't been parents my entire life and now, when I didn't need parents, they decided to step in and play the part. I told them I didn't need them and that I was leaving the second I could and they would never hear from me again. I was a horrible child.

My parents hired two transporters to take me to the wilderness camp. They took me out of the hospital in handcuffs. We had just gotten to the airport when they got the call from my parents telling them to take me home. My words had hit home, and they were taking me back. I flew into Minneapolis, where my parents picked me up and took me home.

I went back to talk to the state's attorney. I honestly tried to be as much help as possible this time. I gave him a notebook with everything I could remember, but I didn't have any of the important details, like names or places. The details I did have were useless. The case didn't look too promising, and one by one all the leads we had were shot down.

And I still wasn't ok. I would wake up from nightmares screaming. I had flashbacks daily. I wasn't eating like I should, and I was self-harming like crazy.

Finally my parents and I together decided I was going back to treatment.

Before I left I had one last task. I wore a hidden microphone and went to talk to the priest that had walked in on us years ago. The detectives sat in a car outside while I went in. I knocked on the door to the priest's office and walked in. We made small talk for a few minutes, but it was awkward. We both knew there was something I needed to say. Then I dropped the bomb.

I asked why he had lied to the police when they asked if he knew about the abuse. He claimed he never knew. I described that day, while he sat there, staring at the ground. He still denied knowing anything. I began to cry, telling him how hard the legal process had been on me. I explained that if only one person would back up my story, it could all go away. He looked me in the eyes and replied, "Jesus suffered too."

Cue my hatred for the Catholic Church. I left there so upset. I got into the car with the detectives absolutely fuming. But there was nothing else to be done. The last lead we had was gone and a few days later I was shipped off to treatment.

Chapter 22

I was a conflicted child.

"No one will ever love you. Just look at the things you've done. Who would ever want you?"

I shake my head, but I know you're right. I'm used. No one will ever love me. You're the only one that will ever want me. Tears fill my eyes as I apologize profusely, promising to never leave you. You nod your head and ask if I love you. I nod and you say, "show me," as you start unbuckling your pants. I drop to my knees.

When you're finished, you pull me to my feet and wipe off my mouth, then hug me, stroking my hair. You tell me how much you love me. How you'll never let anything hurt me. All I can think is, "You just did." But I say nothing.

One of my psychiatrists said that many abuse victims take over where their abusers left off, as was the case with me. Even years after the abuse ended, when I was 17, I sat in her office telling her that I self-harm and have random sex because I don't deserve anything else. When she asked why I told her, "because I'm a bad person," said with a smile of course. She asks me to list some evidence for that statement, and I list off all the things I've done.

She claims the things I did didn't make me a bad person. She tells me I was influenced and or forced to do those things. How I deserve so much better. I just shake my head. She asks what I plan to do with my life and I tell her that I'm going to see him when I turn eighteen. How I plan to apologize for everything I've done to him and put him through. I explain my hope that he will forgive me and he will marry me like he promised, but my fear that he won't. I'm afraid he will hate my guts.

She looks at me and says, "You only think you deserve that because that's what he told you. That's all you grew up with, but Jess, the world is so much bigger than him. You are not beyond repair. You can't change what happened, but you can change where it takes you."

Part of what she said resonated with me, but I still planned on going to see him. I still wanted to be with him.

Chapter 23

I was a broken teen in a safe place.

This time I went to California. Right away I could tell this place was different. The staff legitimately cared about the people in their care. But I was still a scared girl. I became paranoid that my abuser knew my location and was going to come for me. After a week of being in this new home, I ran away. I ended up literally diving into thorny bushes when I was spotted. Eventually I made it to the highway, where I hiked up my skirt, tugged on my shirt, and hitchhiked. Again. Well it didn't take too long for a cop car to pull up beside me. Then another one. Then another. Four cops came out to talk to me. I was terrified. My abuser had told me how the cops would take me away if I ever told what we were doing. So I ran from them. They chased me and tackled me. I was handcuffed, and had a horrible flashback when I was restrained on the gurney to go in the ambulance.

I went to the E.R. The people from the treatment center came and sat with me all night. That was the moment I realized they honestly cared. It wasn't a facade. They sat in the E.R. with me all night instead of going home to their families. They were genuinely concerned about me. And I realized what a major mistake I had made. Immediately I begged to go back, but they weren't sure if they would take me.

I went to the psych ward, again. I was there for around a week. Then I was able to return to my treatment center after signing a contract. Right away, it was hell. I thought I was on one to one supervision. Later I found out it was actually two to one supervision. I couldn't have most of my clothes. Only yoga pants and t-shirts. But I tried not to complain. Little by little I regained trust. Little by little I worked my way through the level system, gaining more privileges. I learned to actually use coping skills. My flashbacks and panic attacks started to occur less and less frequently. I gradually stopped screaming at night. I actually started sleeping. I found a sponsor that I loved and who really understood me.

Eventually I petitioned to the treatment team to become the community leader. This was the highest level. I was then an example, a role model to the other girls, at least that was the idea. And after 103 days, I both happily and sadly left my new home and new family.

Chapter 24

I was finally on the right track.

I went to a day program as a transition from residential treatment to the outside world. It was specifically for eating disorders in Minneapolis. My dad and I stayed in an apartment for a month. Eating was still hard work, but I was able to do it, and they decided I was ready to go back to real life.

Things didn't magically get all better when I left treatment. I had to do a lot of hard work in therapy and outside of it. And everything still wasn't perfect. I still struggled with my eating and self-harm. Occasionally I sexted. But I was trying.

I found a camp for girls that had been sexually abused. I was very hesitant, but I went, and I was so glad I did. I had a blast, and I met Jolene, who became my role model. She put up with my relentless texting and subsided my fears that I was going crazy. I wanted to be just like her, strong, beautiful, and fearless. Together, we deleted the app I used for sexting, and I gave her my blade. She encouraged me to be honest with my therapist, and sat on the phone with me when I called her frantic afterwards. Jolene knew exactly what to say and I related so much to the things she told me. She inspired me to be a better me.

The case against my abuser ended up being dismissed due to lack of evidence. All the times I recanted didn't help things either. When I found out, I panicked. I cried my eyes out and pitied myself. I felt that everything I had gone through was being completely ignored. But then I realized that my experiences were no less real just because the court would never recognize them. It took me time, and it's still a soft spot, but I learned to accept what I could not change, and look at what I could do instead.

I'm obviously not all better. I still have struggles. I still believe that I love him, and deep down, part of him loves me. Is this a defense mechanism like I've been told? Maybe. But it's real to me. I'm still confused about what happened, but I'm only 17. I have time to figure it out, and maybe I never will. I guess I have to just keep taking it one day at a time and eventually I will get where I need to be.

When things get rough, I choose to focus on what I want to become, constantly looking to my role model, Franne. I am a work in progress. I am not a victim and I am not what happened to me. Most importantly, I am not a princess, but what I am is even better. I am free.

Acknowledgements

Where do I even begin? There are so many people that have been so inspirational in my journey. First and foremost: Franne Sippel. Without you, I wouldn't be alive. I don't think you realize the extent to which you've helped me. Sometimes I guess I needed you to call me on my b.s. I so admire you and want to be just like you, but me!

Jolene Loetscher. You helped me realize that I could acknowledge what happened, without letting it define me.

Aja Chavez. Where to begin with you? I am so thankful for you. You taught me to be strong and comfortable in my own skin. Most importantly, you taught me to be comfortable with the calm.

Chris White, Damian Bahr, and everyone else that worked on my case. Thank you. I was a major pain in the you know what, but you put up with me, and tried to understand, even though I definitely did not make it easy for you.

Brittany O'Day. Thank you for all those hours I spent in your office and the time you spent texting me out of my craziness after hours. You put up with me for 12 hours in the car as we went to the child advocacy center, which is amazing!

My family, for being such an amazing support system, and accepting me as I am.

Everyone that I haven't mentioned that has helped me on my journey! (I feel like this is getting a little long). My friends that I met along the way, all my therapists, the people I connected with, thank you. Without you all I would not be who I am today.

Made in the USA
Middletown, DE
18 March 2019